BIRDLAND

A musical drama for soloists, unison voices,
SATB chorus, and instrumental ensemble

Bob Chilcott

STORY AND TEXTS BY CHARLES BENNETT

VOCAL SCORE

MUSIC DEPARTMENT

OXFORD
UNIVERSITY PRESS

OXFORD
UNIVERSITY PRESS

Great Clarendon Street, Oxford OX2 6DP,
United Kingdom

Oxford University Press is a department of the University of Oxford.
It furthers the University's objective of excellence in research, scholarship,
and education by publishing worldwide. Oxford is a registered trade mark of
Oxford University Press in the UK and in certain other countries

© Oxford University Press 2020

Bob Chilcott and Charles Bennett have asserted their right under the Copyright,
Designs and Patents Act, 1988, to be identified as the Authors of this Work

Database right Oxford University Press (maker)

First published 2020

Impression: 1

ISBN 978-0-19-352300-5

Music and text origination by Andrew Jones

Printed in Great Britain on acid-free paper by
Halstan & Co. Ltd, Amersham, Bucks.

Contents

Dramatis Personæ

Pip, a sparrow
Highnote, the Head Bird
Solo Birds 1–4
Solo Doc Rock Peacocks 1–5
Wit (Owl 1)
Woo (Owl 2)
Croakencaw, the Head of the Bewilderness
Shamira, the Golden Nightingale

Unison Chorus Birds
SATB Chorus Birds

All parts can be taken by a high treble voice. The parts of Highnote and Croakencaw can be taken by a high treble voice or a broken male voice.

Instrumentation

Flute
2 clarinets in B♭
Horn in F
Trumpet in B♭
Tenor trombone
Percussion (2 players)
Bass guitar (or double bass)
Piano

Also available:
Birdland Rehearsal Pack (ISBN 978–0–19–354015–6)

    – Photocopiable unison part

    – Photocopiable lyric sheets

    – Access to a companion website, featuring downloadable audio rehearsal tracks and unison part and lyric sheets for printing

Composer's note

The poet Charles Bennett and I had for quite some time discussed the possibility of writing an extended dramatic work for young singers. Charles had the basis of the story in his mind, and we agreed that we wanted to write a piece not only about singing but also about what it means to have the courage to sing with your own voice, thus ultimately being true to who you really are. We were thrilled when Jon Cullen from Magdalen College School in Oxford, alongside Lucy Farrant from the Young Norfolk Arts Trust and Alison Corfield from Norfolk Music Hub, agreed to be partners with us by commissioning this piece. Thus *Birdland* came to life and received its first performances concurrently in the summer of 2020 at the Oxford Festival of the Arts and at the Young Norfolk Arts Festival, in Norwich Theatre Royal.

For us a major consideration was to make the piece as flexible for performance as we could. We have tried to make the solo roles interchangeable, in that they can be sung by any voice part. Even though the piece is fundamentally designed for young singers, the solo roles can equally be sung by adults or by young voices and adult voices combined. The work is scored for an ensemble of ten players, but it can also be performed with just piano or piano with the help of percussion and bass guitar or double bass. In the same way we have tried not to be too prescriptive about stage directions. Even though we have tried to imagine the temporal shape and pacing of the piece through the scoring and narrative, we hope that there will be plenty of scope for creative staging. We imagined that the piece could include dance and movement, from the possibility of an occasional dancing chorus to perhaps a more formal dance routine in movement eight, 'Downwards.' We hope that, ultimately, the nature of the piece might be able to stimulate and encourage as imaginative and broad a palette of ideas as possible, when bringing it to life.

As well as the commissioners, I would like to thank a number of colleagues who have helped this piece come to life. Thanks are due to Val Withams from Choral Connections and also to Griselda Sherlaw-Johnson and Jenny Wegg at Oxford University Press. I would especially like to thank our editor, Laura Jones, for her tireless work on this piece, not only for her careful work on the score but also for her masterminding of all the learning materials for the work, which she has done with grace, good humour, and endless patience.

Bob Chilcott
November 2019

Duration: *c*.45 mins

This note may be reproduced as required for programme notes.

BIRDLAND

Charles Bennett (b. 1954)

BOB CHILCOTT

1. Prologue
(*Pip, SATB Chorus Birds*)

SCENE 1—Early morning in Birdland. Pip is awake, standing centre stage.

PIP
My fea-thers are brown, but what col-our is my voice? You could lis-ten to a rain-bow,_____ if you

Printed in Great Britain

OXFORD UNIVERSITY PRESS, MUSIC DEPARTMENT, GREAT CLARENDON STREET, OXFORD OX2 6DP

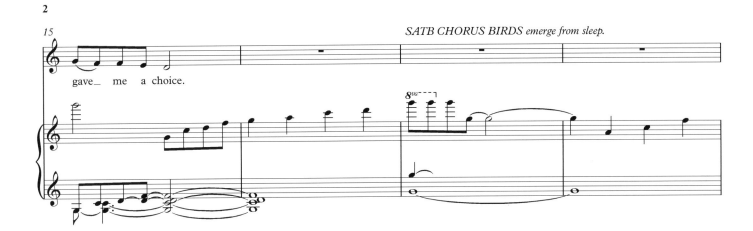

SATB CHORUS BIRDS emerge from sleep.

gave__ me a choice.

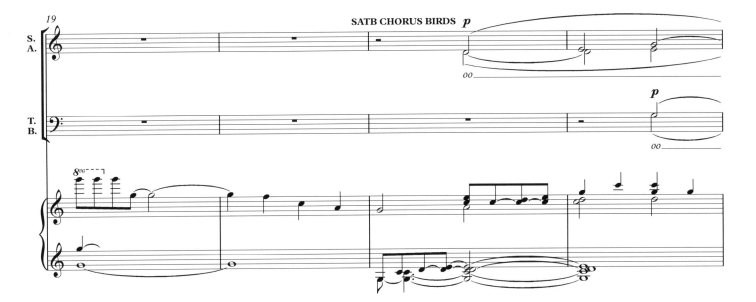

SATB CHORUS BIRDS *p*

oo

p

oo

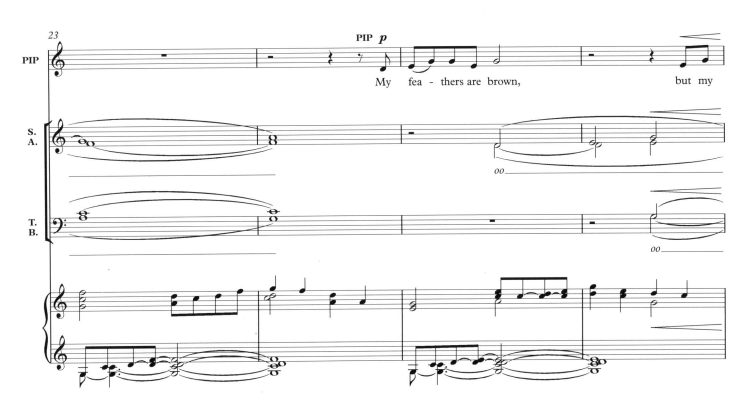

PIP *p*

My fea - thers are brown, but my

oo

oo

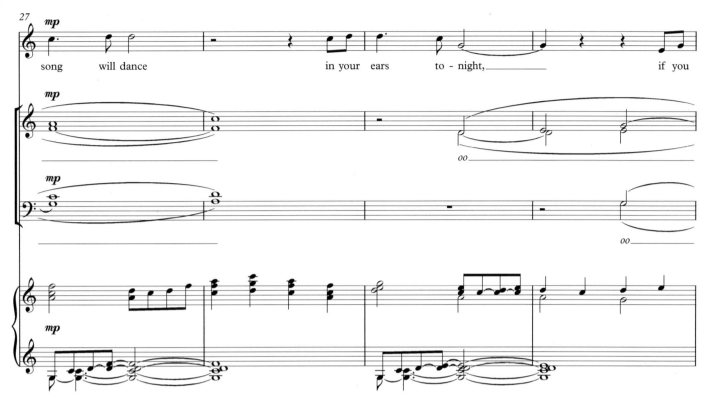

song will dance in your ears to - night,_____ if you

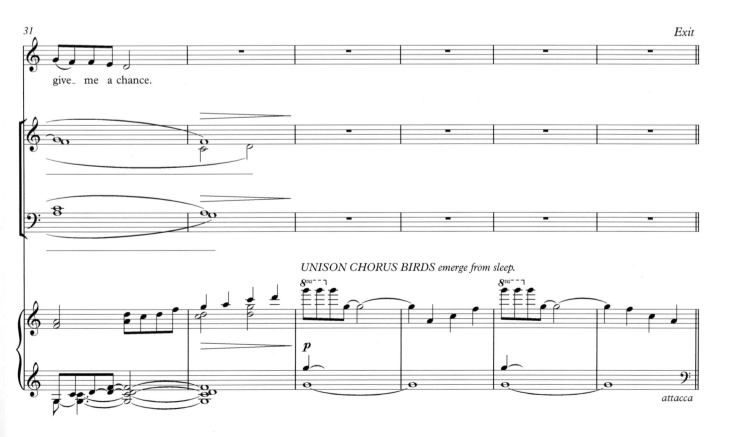

give_ me a chance.

Exit

UNISON CHORUS BIRDS *emerge from sleep.*

attacca

2. One Note
(Unison Chorus Birds, SATB Chorus Birds)

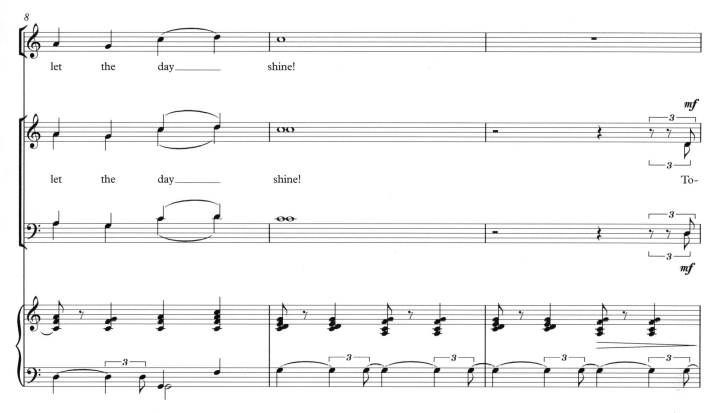

let the day_____ shine!

let the day_____ shine!   To-

- mor-row you know is Mid-sum-mer's Day, the ve - ry best birds will have their say.   But

what can I tell you? Life is rough. Not ev-'ry bird is good e-nough!

One note, to be-gin, let the ___ light in. One note, now's the time,

One note, to be-gin, let the ___ light in. One note, now's the time,

let the day_____ shine!   On

let the day_____ shine!

UNISON VOICES

Mid-sum-mer's Day we'll sing at dawn a con - cert as the morn - ing's born.   But

what can I tell you? Things are tough. Not ev - 'ry bird can strut their stuff!

8

One note, to be-gin, let the light in. One note, now's the time,

One note, to be-gin, let the light in. One note, now's the time,

let the day___ shine!

let the day___ shine! Se -

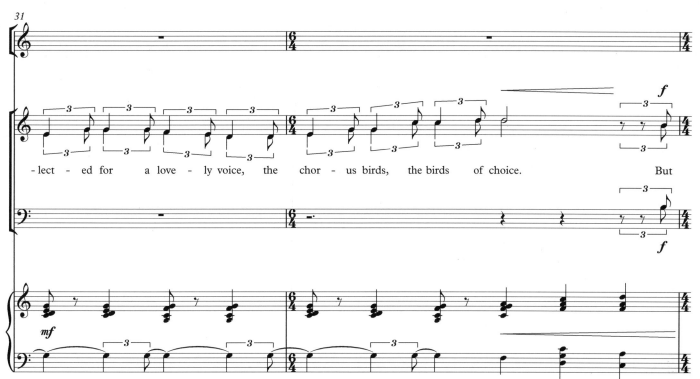

-lect -ed for a love - ly voice, the chor - us birds, the birds of choice. But

what can I tell you? (Not a word.) There are birds, should not be heard!

One note, to be-gin, let the___ light in.

One note, to be-gin, let the___ light in.

One note, now's the time, let the day, the day___ shine!

One note, now's the time, let the day, the day___ shine!

Let the day shine, let the

Let the day shine, let the

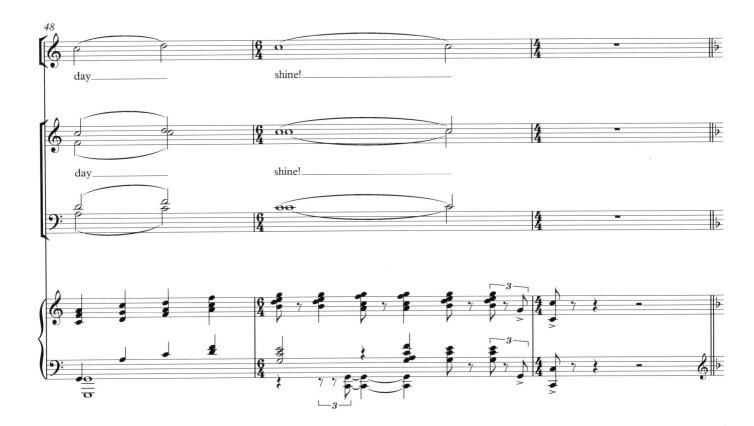

day shine!

day shine!

3. *Feathered Perfection*
(*Highnote, Solo Birds*)

SOLO BIRD 3

SOLO BIRD 4

It's not our fault we're the best.

It's the dream of ev - 'ry bird.

SOLO BIRDS 3 & 4

ALL SOLO BIRDS

And that's us!

And that's____ us!

We're

fea-thered per - fec - tion,

And that's us!

HIGHNOTE
"And remember, we have to make sure that our ineffable beauty of song keeps the wannabees and aspiring singers out of the running for ever.

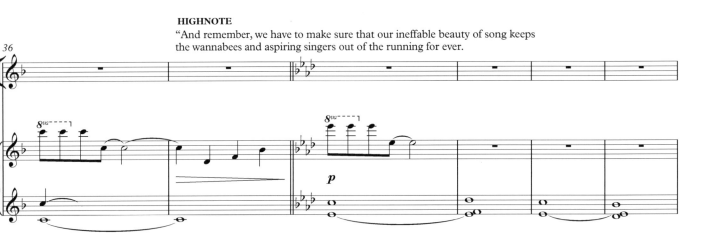

Just one false note, one wrong step, one feather out of place
and aeons of natural selection would go up in smoke."

15

16

HIGHNOTE

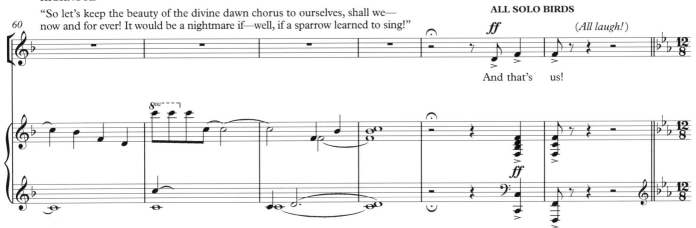

"So let's keep the beauty of the divine dawn chorus to ourselves, shall we—
now and for ever! It would be a nightmare if—well, if a sparrow learned to sing!"

ALL SOLO BIRDS

(All laugh!)

And that's us!

4. You'll never believe it

(Solo Bird, Unison Chorus Birds, SATB Chorus Birds)

Woke this mor-ning, felt so bad._____ Had the worst night-mare

I've ev-er had._____ You'll ne-ver be-lieve it, here's the thing,___

Dreamt last night a spar-row_could

SATB CHORUS BIRDS

sing. What's

that we heard? What's that you said?_____ Wish we were still a -

18

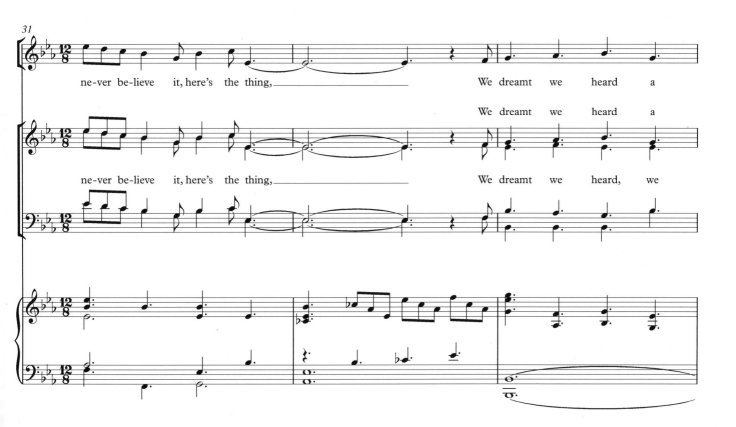

spar - row sing!
spar - row sing!
heard a spar - row sing!

sub. *mf*

mf

To - mor-row at dawn, you re - al - ise,____

mf

sang in - stead. You'll ne-ver be-lieve it; Oh, the dread!_____

Oh, the dread!_____

sang in - stead. You'll ne-ver be-lieve it; Oh, the dread, the dread!_____

If a spar - row sang____ in - stead.

If a spar - row sang____ in - stead.

5. I have a song

(*Pip, Unison Chorus Birds, SATB Chorus Birds, Highnote*)

39

No one must ev - er hear a sound so pain - ful, so pain - ful to the ear.

No one must ev - er hear a sound so pain - ful, so pain - ful to the ear.

42

(shout)

NE - VER! NE - VER NE - VER NE - VER! NE - VER! NE - VER!

No one must ev - er hear a sound so pain - ful, so pain - ful to the ear.

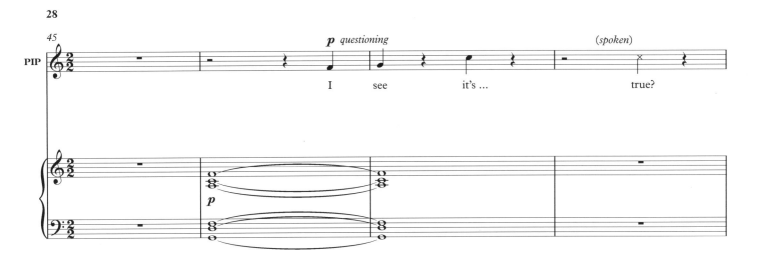

45

PIP

p questioning

(spoken)

I   see   it's …   true?

p

HIGHNOTE (*ripe with condescension, mock-friendly*)

"Come closer, my little, insignificant, tiny, small, inconsequential one. You've managed to achieve something quite extraordinary: a musical disaster of unprecedented proportions."

6. It's natural to dream
(Highnote, Pip, SATB Chorus Birds)

Gentle tempo, but sung with menace ♩ = 66

p

mp

5

HIGHNOTE

p

3   *3*   *mp*

It's nat-ural to dream,   my lit-tle one,   But ug - ly duck-lings don't

p   *mp*

turn in-to swans. And though we sym-pa-thise with you, my love, A

ra-ven ne-ver turns in-to a dove.

PIP
"All beginners make mistakes."

PIP
"I'll promise to do whatever it takes."

HIGHNOTE *mp*
You're not__ the first who wants to

SATB CHORUS BIRDS *p*
oo_____ oo_____
oo_____

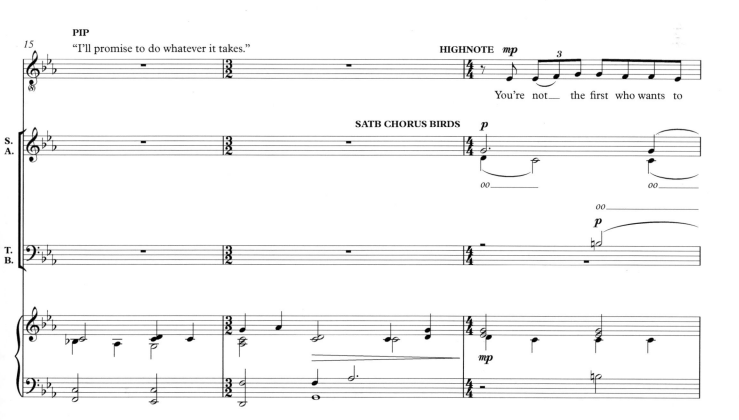

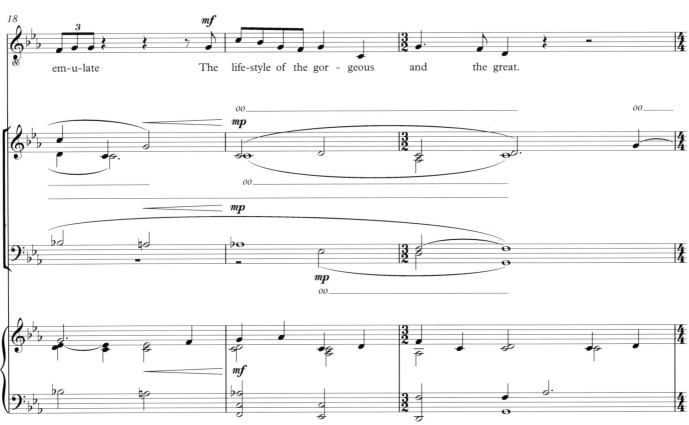

em-u-late   The life-style of the gor - geous   and   the great.

But hon-est - ly, we have to tell   you true: We'll sing, you do what-ev-er it is you do.

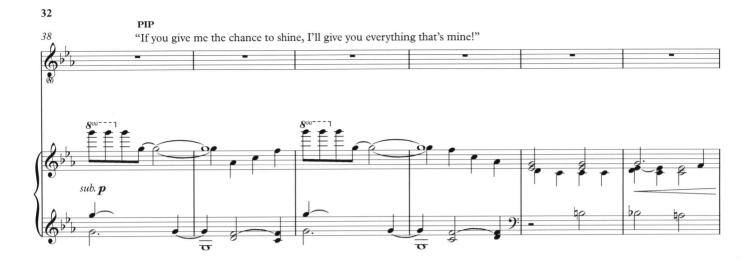

PIP
"If you give me the chance to shine, I'll give you everything that's mine!"

HIGHNOTE

That's what I ra - ther hoped you'd say,

So just sign here with - out de - lay.   We'll see_ some friends of ours who'll make A

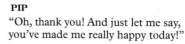

PIP
"Oh, thank you! And just let me say,
you've made me really happy today!"

star from an un - tal - ent - ed mis - take.

(signs contract) **rit.**

HIGHNOTE

"Don't mention it! It's my duty and my pleasure to take you where you can get the professional help you so very badly need, my little, tiny speck of easily overlooked, not-very-interesting dust."

PIP

"Thank you. Lovely.
Marvellous. Great. Where to?"

HIGHNOTE

"The Doc Rock Peacocks. You must have heard of them. They can fix any problem, great, or, as in your case, very, very small. They can build reputations and tear them down. They made Shamira, the Golden Nightingale, the fabled, block-busting star of stage and screen and national treasure she is today!"

34

7. Make that dream come true
(Pip, Unison Chorus Birds)

8. Downwards
(*SATB Chorus Birds*)

Journeying to the Bower of Power, the home of the Doc Rock Peacocks

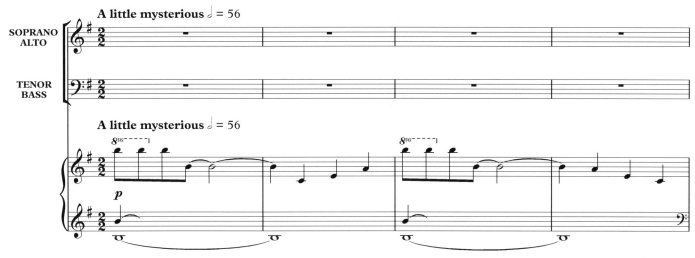

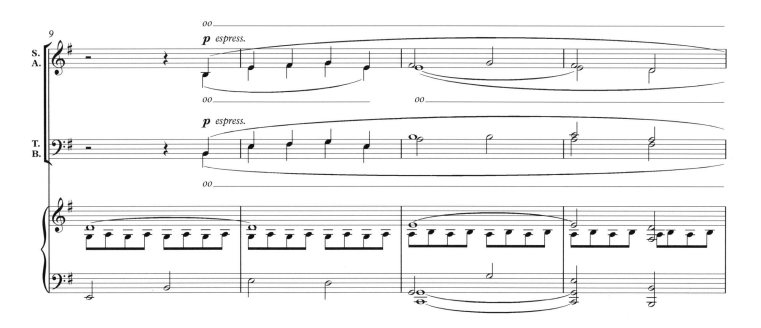

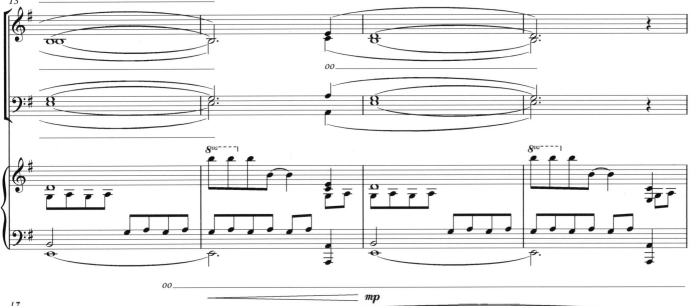

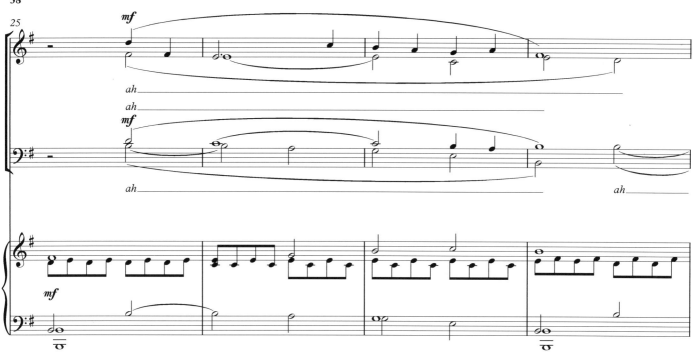

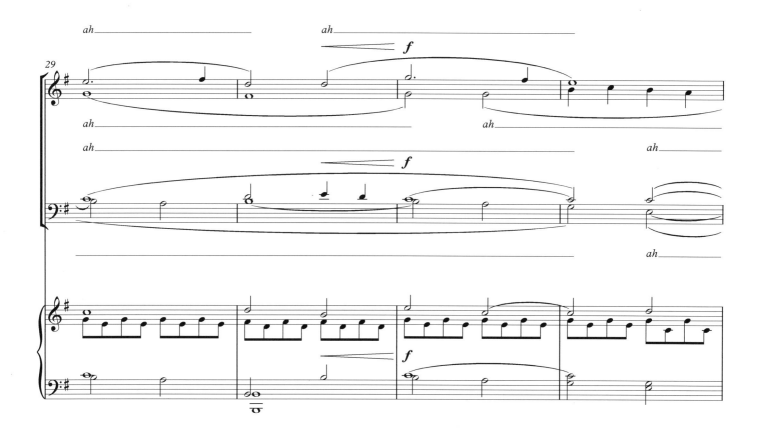

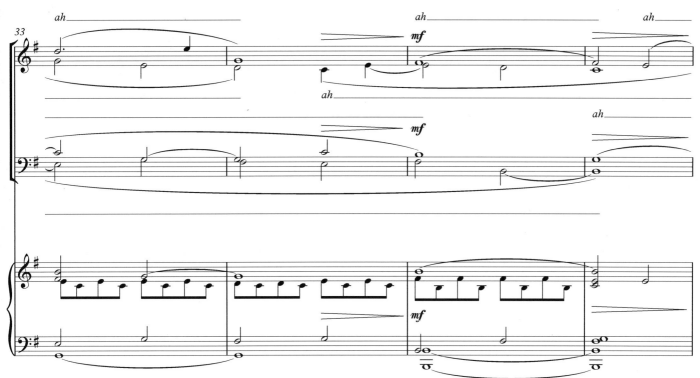

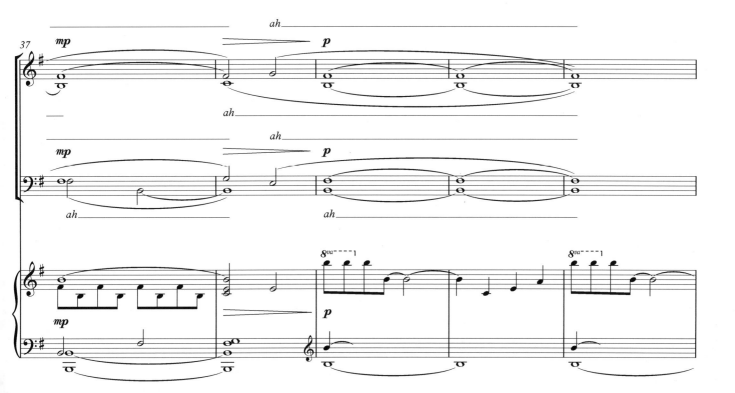

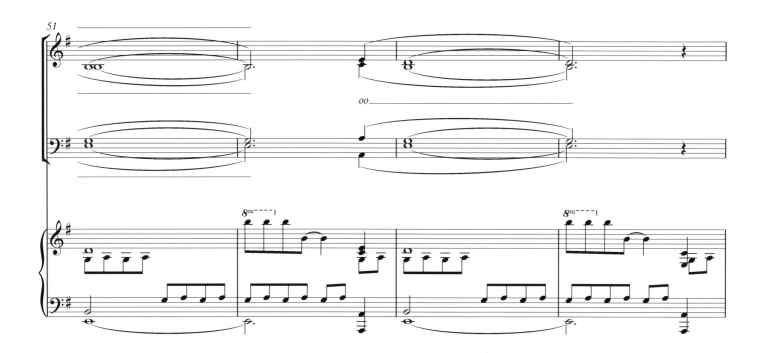

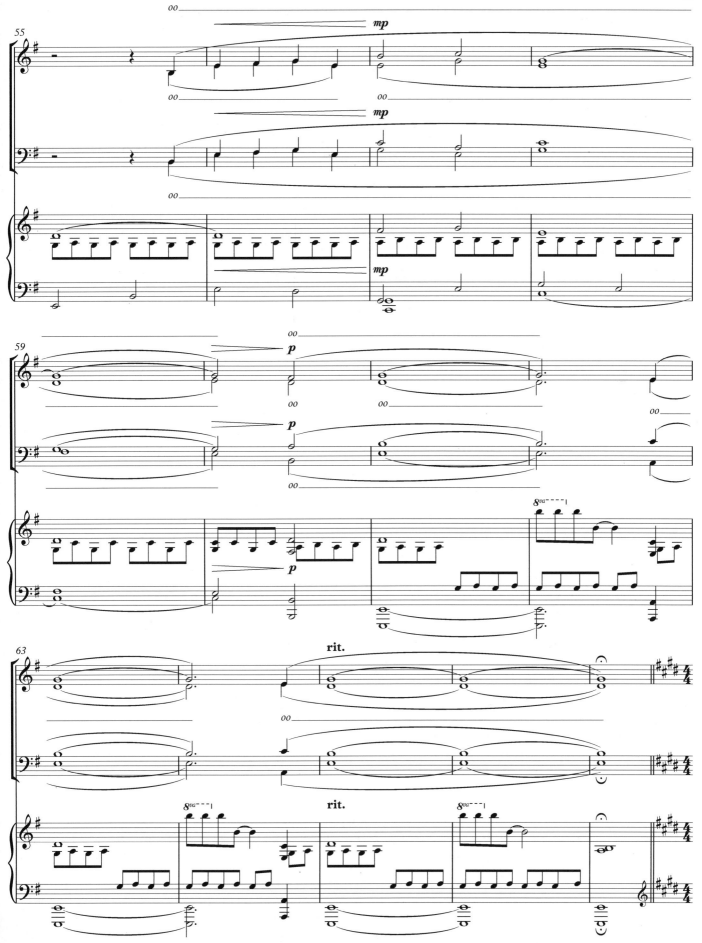

9. The Bower of Power
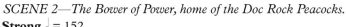
(Unison Chorus Birds, SATB Chorus Birds, Pip, Highnote, Solo Doc Rock Peacocks)

SCENE 2—The Bower of Power, home of the Doc Rock Peacocks.

We can make it bet-ter, what-ev - er you're feel - ing._____ When

We can make it bet-ter, what-ev - er you're feel - ing._____ When

song goes wrong it's time___ to come a - long And let the Doc___ Rocks fix___

song goes wrong it's time___ to come a - long And let the Doc___ Rocks fix___

of heal - ing. We can make it bet - ter, what - ev - er you're feel - ing.

When song goes wrong it's time to come a - long And

let the Doc___ Rocks fix_____ you   with a lit - tle bag of

let the Doc___ Rocks fix_____ you   with a lit - tle bag of

PIP
"Yes, I think I'd like to."

DOC ROCK PEACOCK 1
"Yes, we recommend something other people in your
situation tend to need—a sort of back-to-basics plan."

UNIS.

tricks!

S.
A.

tricks!

T.
B.

mp

* Repeat as necessary, following the narration.

ALL DOC ROCK PEACOCKS

"WE'LL TEAR YOU DOWN
AND BUILD YOU UP AGAIN!"

S.
A.

46 unis. **mf**

Af - ter all, dear spar - row, on your own you'd sure - ly fail   If you tried to war - ble like the

T.
B.

unis.

mf

mf

Gold - en Night - in - gale.   She's our great - est tri - umph,   our o - ver-night suc - cess.   The

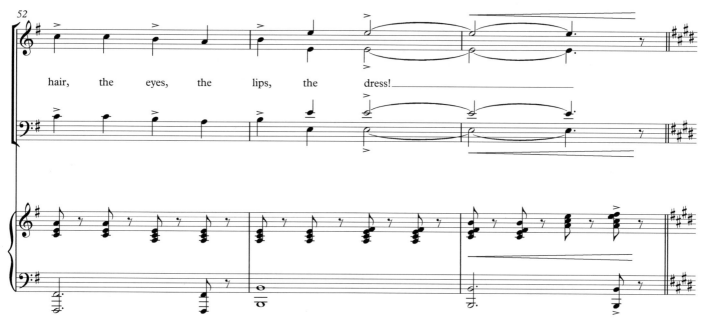

hair, the eyes, the lips, the dress!_____

UNIS. Wel-come to the Bower__ of Power. Wel-come to the place__

S. A. Wel-come to the Bower__ of Power. Wel-come to the place__

T. B.

of heal - ing. We can make it bet - ter, what - ev - er you're feel - ing._____

of heal - ing. We can make it bet - ter, what - ev - er you're feel - ing._____

When song goes wrong it's time___ to come a - long And

When song goes wrong it's time___ to come a - long And

DOC ROCK PEACOCK 2

"Take the next step. Certainly. You're sure? We'll pry and probe and make you what you never were before. We'll break you and remake you in an image of our own."

x 2

PIP

"Perhaps I might just ..."

let the Doc Rocks fix you   with a lit - tle bag of

let the Doc Rocks fix you   with a lit - tle bag of

UNIS.

tricks!

S.
A.

tricks!

T.
B.

mp

ALL DOC ROCK PEACOCKS

"THEY WON'T RECOGNISE YOU BACK HOME!"

Now let's have a look at you: has-n't he done well! Trans - formed com-plete - ly

un - der our spell. There's just a few more things to rem-ed - y and tweak: The

53

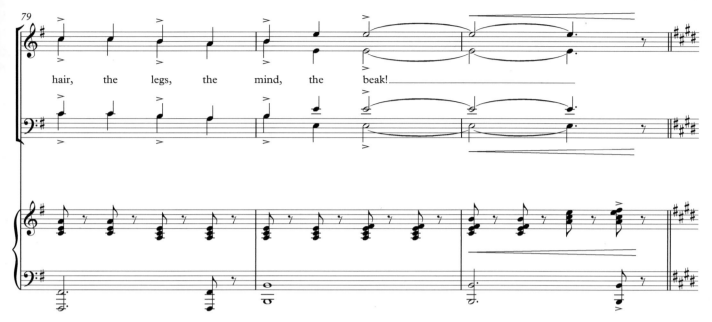

hair,   the   legs,   the   mind,   the   beak!

Wel-come   to the Bower_ of Power.   Wel-come   to the place_

Wel-come   to the Bower_ of Power.   Wel-come   to the place_

of heal - ing. We can make it bet - ter, what - ev - er you're feel - ing.

of heal - ing. We can make it bet - ter, what - ev - er you're feel - ing.

When song goes wrong it's time to come a - long And

When song goes wrong it's time to come a - long And

let the Doc__ Rocks fix_____ you   with a lit‑tle bag of

let the Doc__ Rocks fix_____ you   with a lit‑tle bag of

PIP
"But I thought ..."

DOC ROCK PEACOCK 3
"I'm afraid, dear sparrow, there we disagree.
And did we mention (since we're on a roll)?"

UNIS.

tricks!

S.
A.

tricks!

T.
B.

* Repeat as necessary, following the narration.

56

of heal - ing. We can make it bet - ter, what - ev - er you're feel - ing.

of heal - ing. We can make it bet - ter, what - ev - er you're feel - ing.

Make it bet - ter, what - ev - er you're feel - ing.

When song goes wrong it's time to come a - long And

When song goes wrong it's time to come a - long And

let the Doc Rocks fix____ you,   fix you.

let the Doc Rocks fix____ you,   fix you.

with a lit - tle bag of tricks!

with a lit - tle bag of tricks!

10. Time to move on

(SATB Chorus Birds, Pip, Unison Chorus Birds, Solo Doc Rock Peacocks 1–3)

We've done what we could to make him a star, But still he re-sist-ed, per-

-haps we went too far. Now there is no-thing more we can do.

Time__ to move on to some - thing new.__

Time__ to move on to some - thing new.

Time__ to move on to some - thing new.

You'll__ ne-ver do it on__ your own.

64

-wards your des - ti - ny.___   Now there is   no - thing more   we___ can do. __

Time__ to move on   to some - thing new.___

Time__ to move on   to some - thing new.___

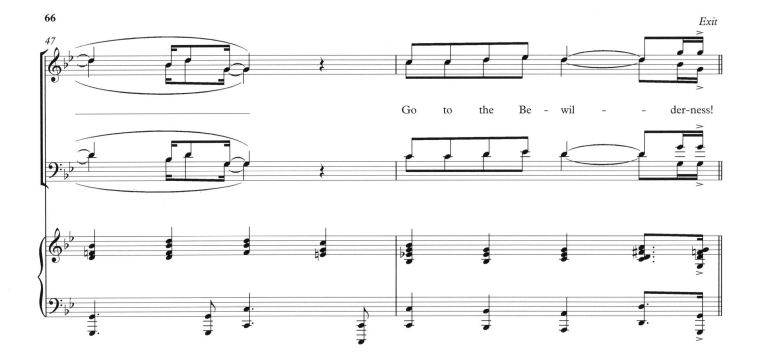

Go to the Be - wil - - - der-ness!

Colla voce ♩ = 76

PIP
"But what is the Bewilderness?"

DOC ROCK PEACOCK 1
"A place of unheard notes."

DOC ROCK PEACOCK 2
"Notes that have no music."

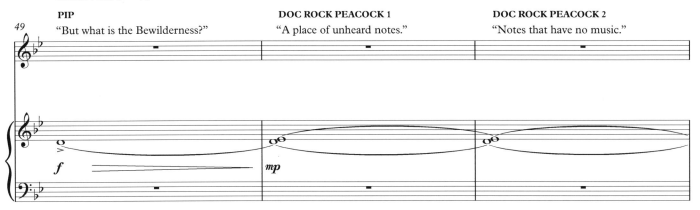

DOC ROCK PEACOCK 3
"Music that has no time."

PIP
"What will I do there?"

DOC ROCK PEACOCK 1
"Dance without movement."

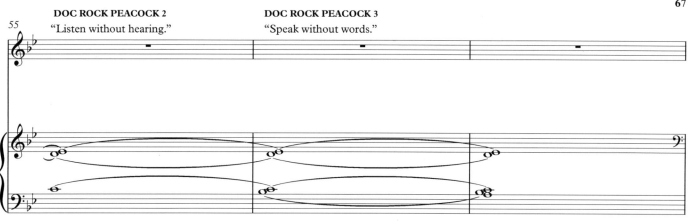

DOC ROCK PEACOCK 2
"Listen without hearing."

DOC ROCK PEACOCK 3
"Speak without words."

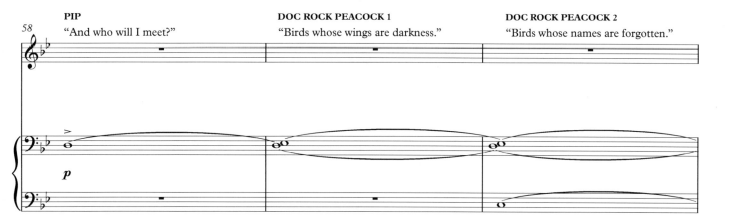

PIP
"And who will I meet?"

DOC ROCK PEACOCK 1
"Birds whose wings are darkness."

DOC ROCK PEACOCK 2
"Birds whose names are forgotten."

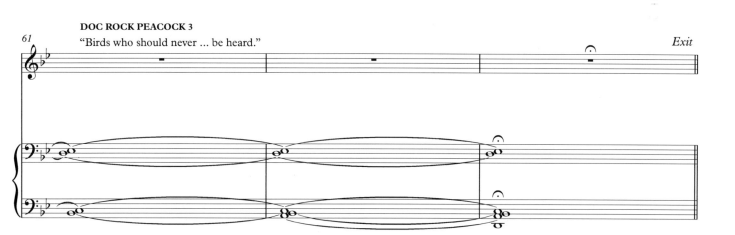

DOC ROCK PEACOCK 3
"Birds who should never ... be heard."

Exit

PIP

"Is what I wanted so wrong? To sing my own song. Is there a way to make it clear? The notes I hear? How can what's inside of me see the light of day? I thought I had music. Has it gone away?"

68

11. Owl Talk
(Wit, Woo, Pip, Croakencaw)

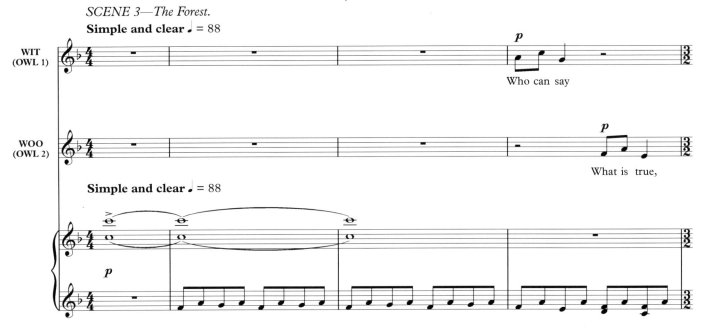

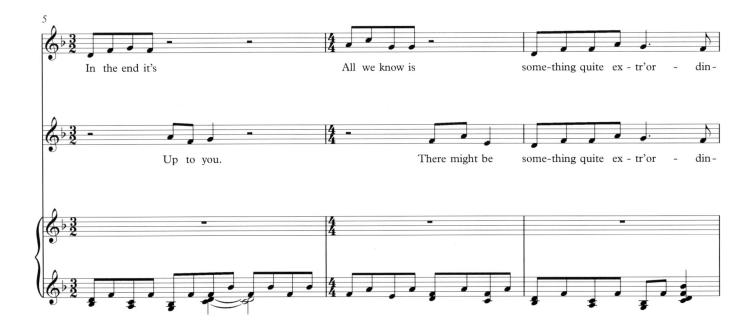

70

26

And the Be - wil - der - ness   Comes to   you!

Comes to   you!

PIP
"Well, I feel utterly lost! It's all hopeless. Now I'll never sing like the Golden Nightingale."

29

WIT
"Oh, we know a thing or two about her."   "Things that would make you
see her ..."

WOO
"Oh yes. We could tell you things
that would blow your wings off."   "... In a totally different light."

(WIT)
"We saw how the Doc Rock Peacocks made her!"

35

mf

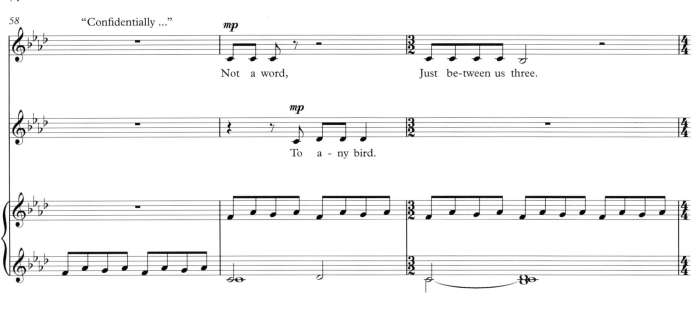

CROAKENCAW

"Hello, hello, hello. What stranger have we here?"

PIP

"Only a sparrow who thought he could sing. Only a sparrow with a broken wing."

CROAKENCAW

"Come with me. You'll fit in beautifully down here. Where the forest is dark and drear. Where your dreams don't mean a thing. You're the bird who could not sing."

12. The Bewilderness

(Croakencaw, SATB Chorus Birds, Pip)

SCENE 4—The Bewilderness.

Heavy and dark ♩ = 72

CROAKENCAW "The Bewilderness finds everyone like us in the end. The croakers, the broken, the rotten, the forgotten."

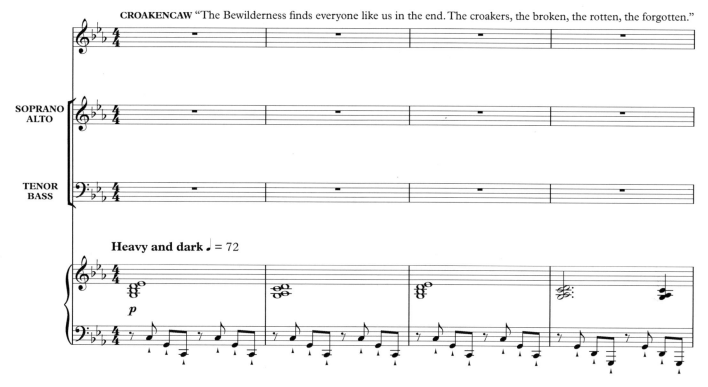

CROAKENCAW   PIP

"It takes us when no one else will."   "But who are you, and what do you call yourselves?"   "Birds who made bad choices."

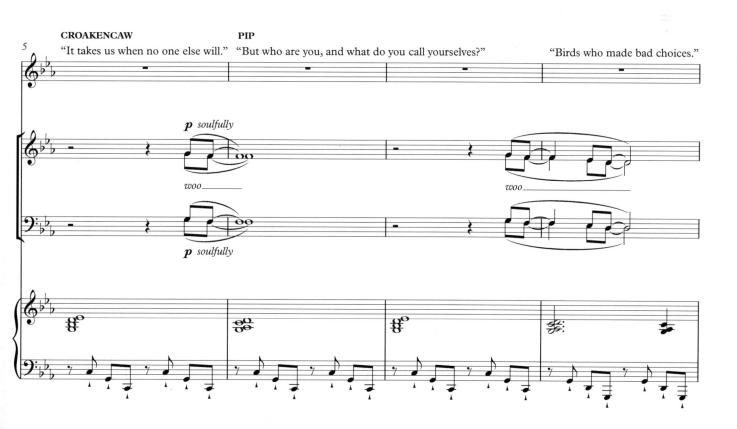

CROAKENCAW

"Birds whose names are dirty words.   Birds who should never ... be heard."

din - gy,   ev -'ry-thing that's drear,   Ev -'ry-thing that's bro - ken   winds up

* 'Maggot pie' = magpie

78

With our voice of dark-ness, we will raise_____ a cheer. Fail-ures such as you add to

our_____ suc-cess. Soon you'll learn to live in the Be - wil-der-ness,_____ Be -

-wil-der-ness._____

woo_____

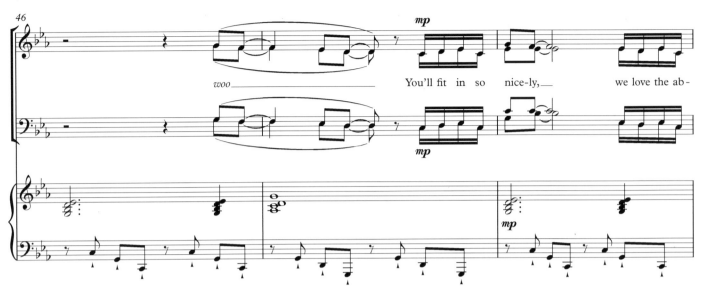

woo_____ You'll fit in so nice-ly,___ we love the ab-

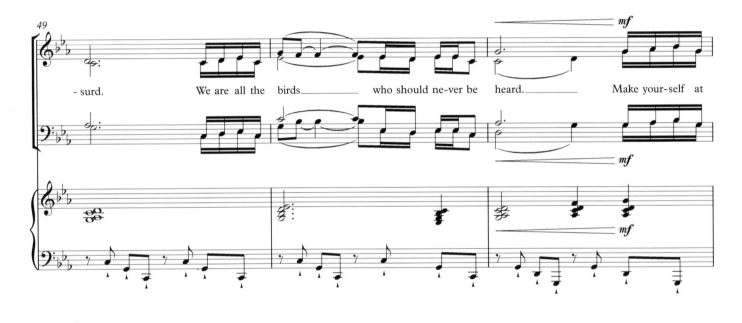

- surd. We are all the birds_____ who should ne-ver be heard._____ Make your-self at

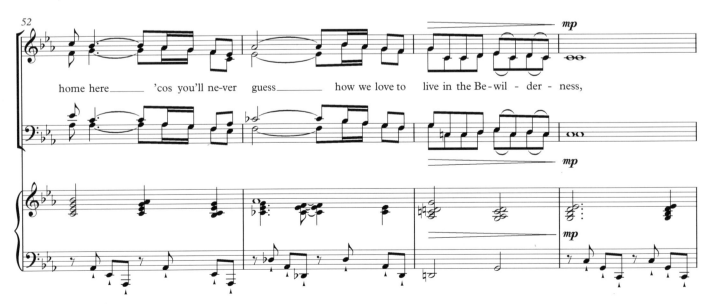

home here_____ 'cos you'll ne-ver guess_____ how we love to live in the Be-wil - der - ness,

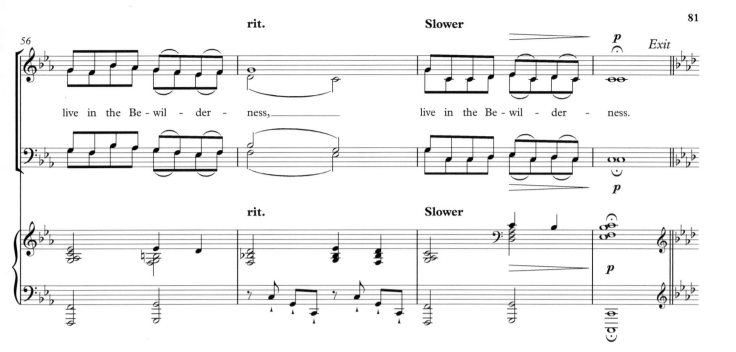

live in the Be - wil - der - ness,_____ live in the Be - wil - der - ness.

13. Owl Talk again
(Wit, Woo, Shamira, Pip)

SCENE 5—*The Forest. Night. Pip comes centre stage and sleeps.*

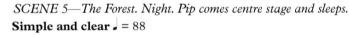

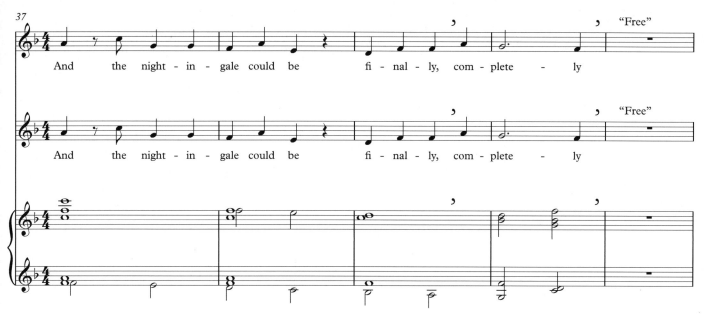

And the night - in - gale could be fi - nal - ly, com - plete - ly "Free"

And the night - in - gale could be fi - nal - ly, com - plete - ly "Free"

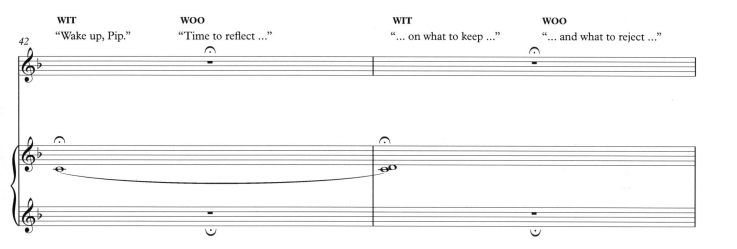

WIT   **WOO**   **WIT**   **WOO**
"Wake up, Pip."   "Time to reflect ..."   "... on what to keep ..."   "... and what to reject ..."

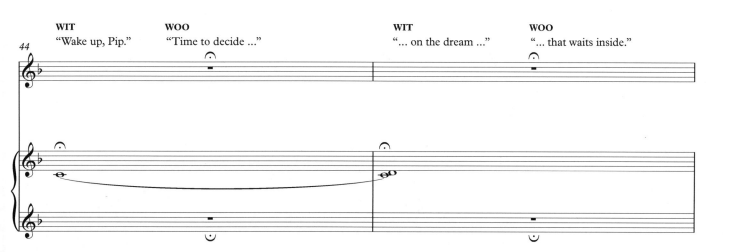

WIT   **WOO**   **WIT**   **WOO**
"Wake up, Pip."   "Time to decide ..."   "... on the dream ..."   "... that waits inside."

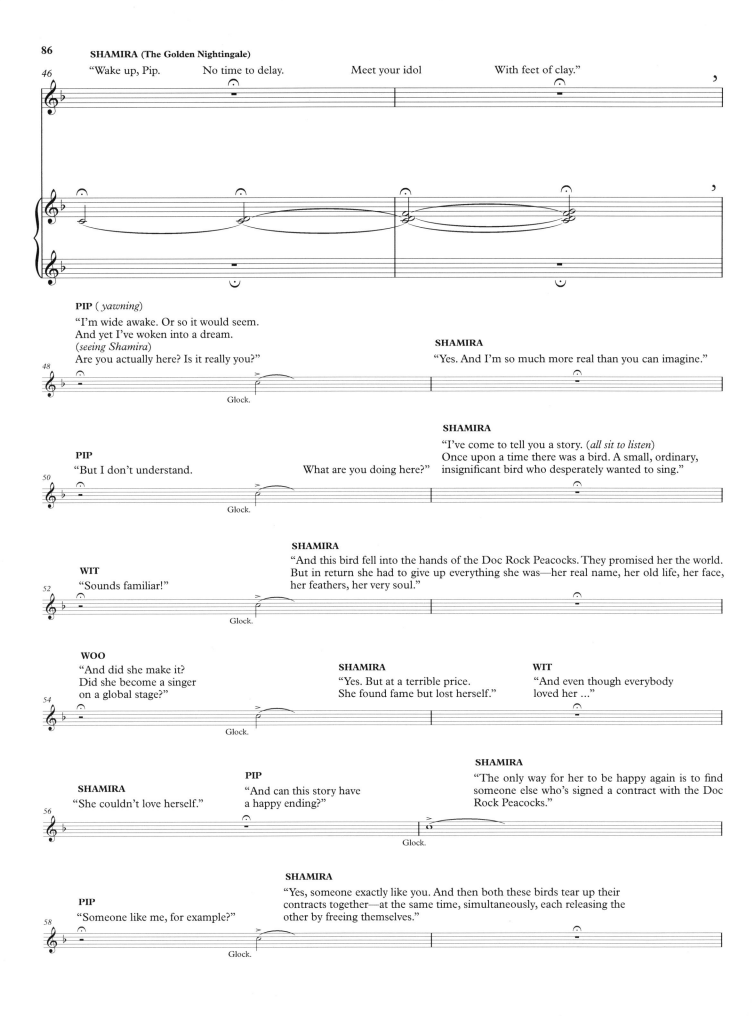

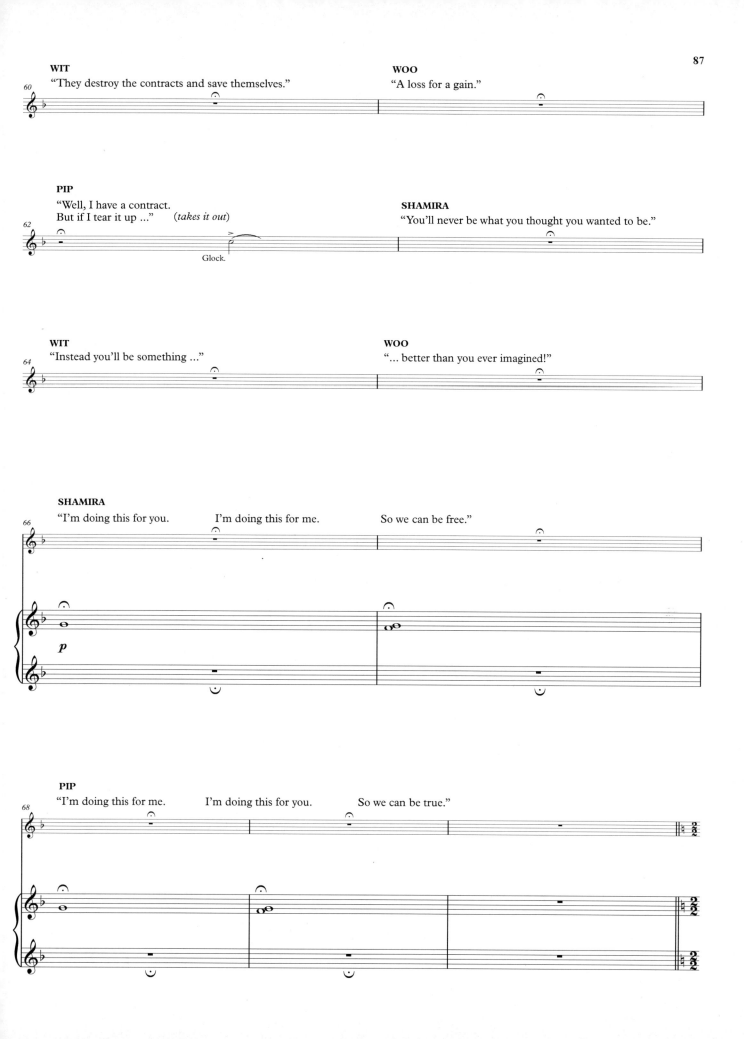

14. Dream Vision

(Shamira, Pip)

am your dream vi - sion come to tell you true. Lis - ten to the
2. Let me share my se - cret in this wak - ing dream: I am not pre -

mu - sic deep in - side of you. Lis - ten to___ it whis - per,
-cise - ly gold - en as I seem. Un - der-neath these fea - thers,

whis-per in_ your ear,_ Fill-ing you_____ with joy in - stead of fear.

I'm the same as you._

Un - der-neath I'm like a spar-row too._____ Now, my luck - y

spar - row, now you have the chance. Wake up to the mu - sic and your

song will dance. Time to be_ a he - ro, time to be_ a

star. Wake up now to who you real-ly are, you

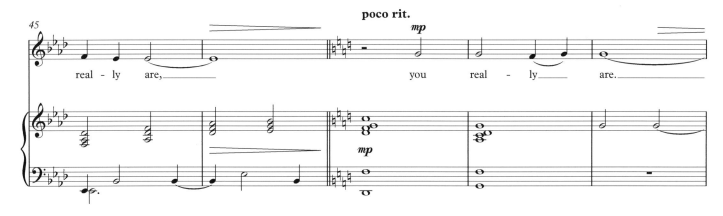

real-ly are, you real-ly are.

Like a fea-ther on the wind, like the dawn-ing of the day, I

(SHAMIRA)

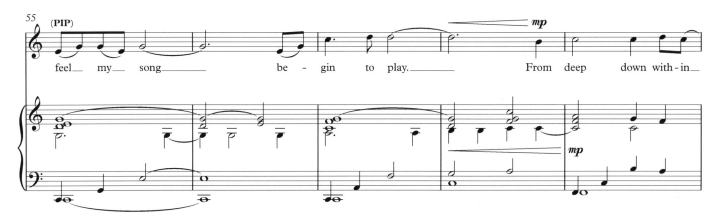

feel my song be-gin to play. From deep down with-in

UNISON CHORUS and SATB CHORUS BIRDS slowly begin to
gather on stage. They listen in amazement to the singing.

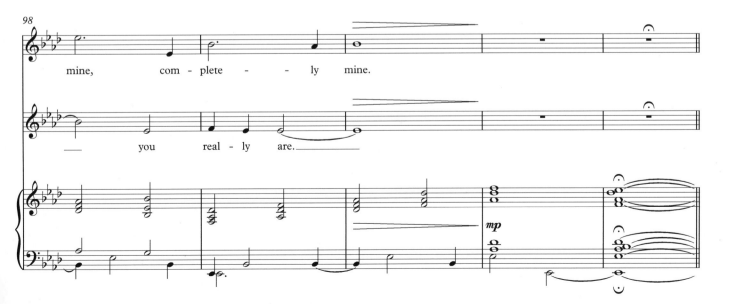

94

15. The Music of Light
(Pip, Shamira, Unison Chorus Birds, SATB Chorus Birds, Highnote)

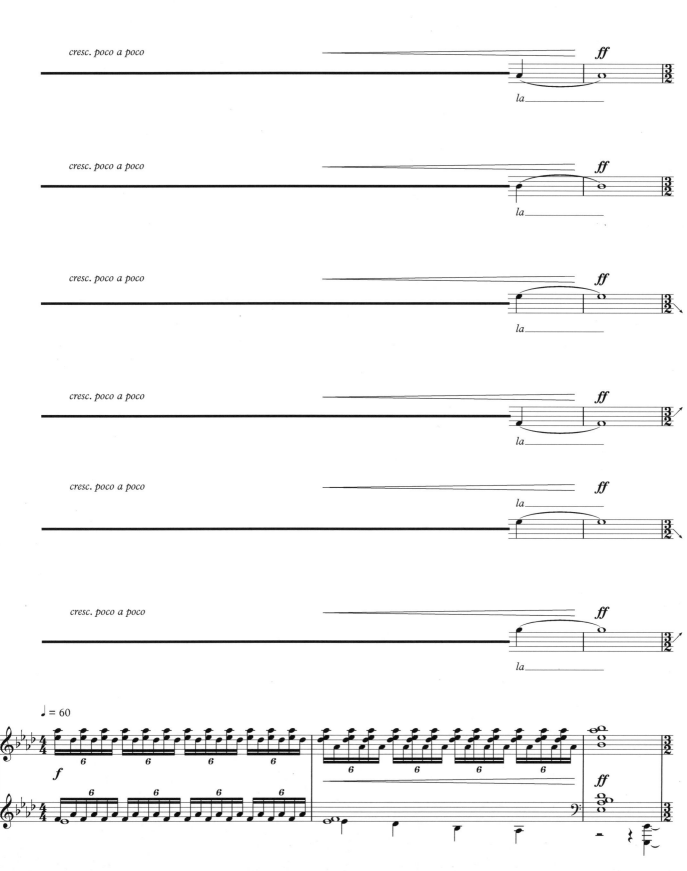

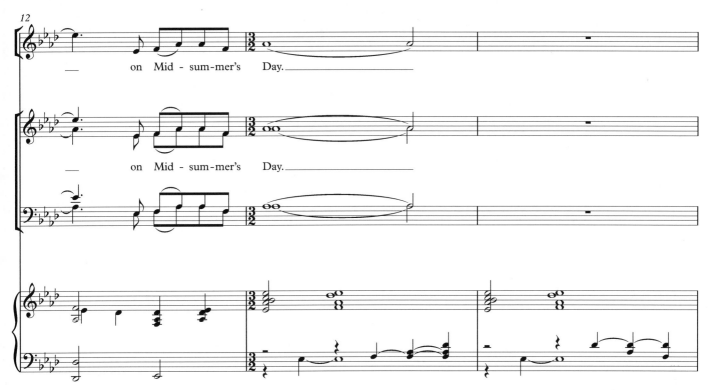

on Mid - sum-mer's Day.

on Mid - sum-mer's Day.

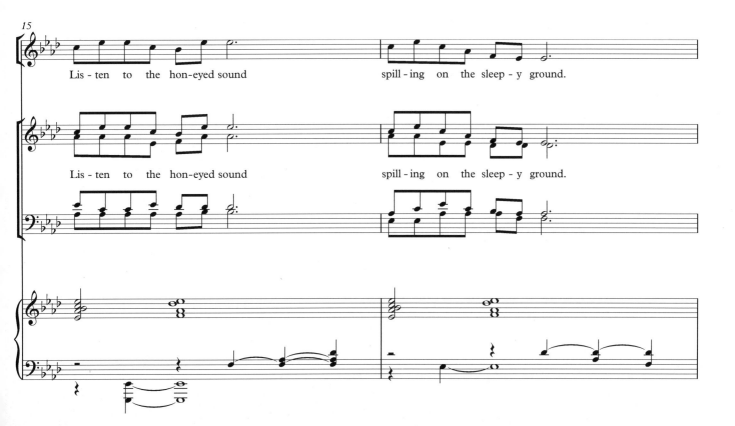

Lis - ten to the hon-eyed sound   spill - ing on the sleep - y ground.

Lis - ten to the hon-eyed sound   spill - ing on the sleep - y ground.

Greet the sun and let it play the mu - sic of light

Greet the sun and let it play the mu - sic of light, of

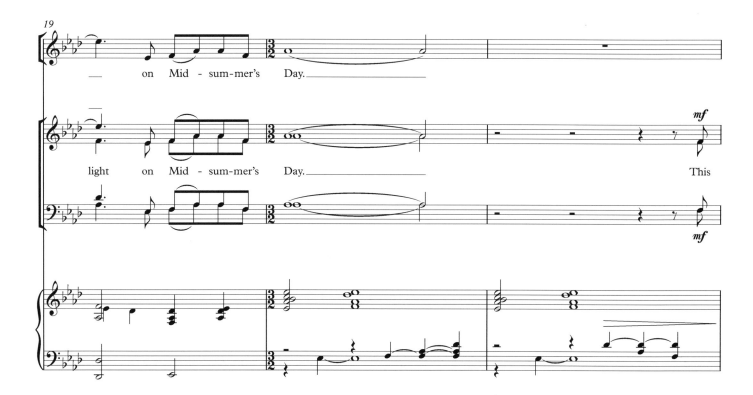

on Mid - sum - mer's Day.

light on Mid - sum - mer's Day. This

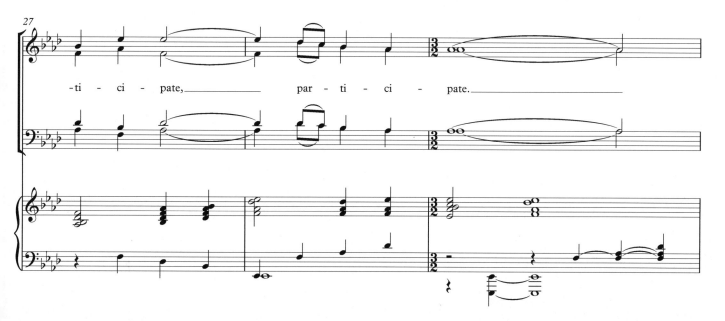

HIGHNOTE (*sheds a tear*)

"That's the best dawn chorus I've ever heard. It makes me really proud to be a bird! Well done, everyone. I never thought I'd say this, but the dawn chorus isn't just for a few. It actually sounds better than ever before. From now on, everyone can sing. Well, I think we learnt a valuable lesson today ..."

ALL

"Oh do shut up!"

16. *One Note (reprise)*

(Unison Chorus Birds, SATB Chorus Birds)

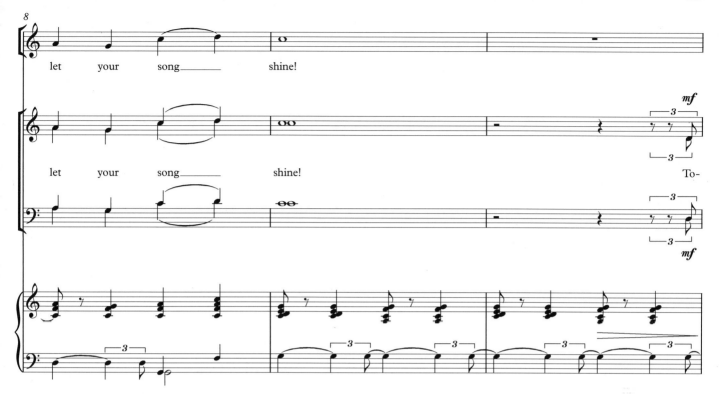

let your song____ shine!

let your song____ shine!

To-

-day as you know is Mid-sum-mer's Day, when all the birds may have their say.

let your song_____ shine!

let your song_____ shine!

We

hear the beau - ty of your voice, we ce - le-brate, we all re-joice!

Now we can tell you (not a word), all kinds of songs, they must be heard!

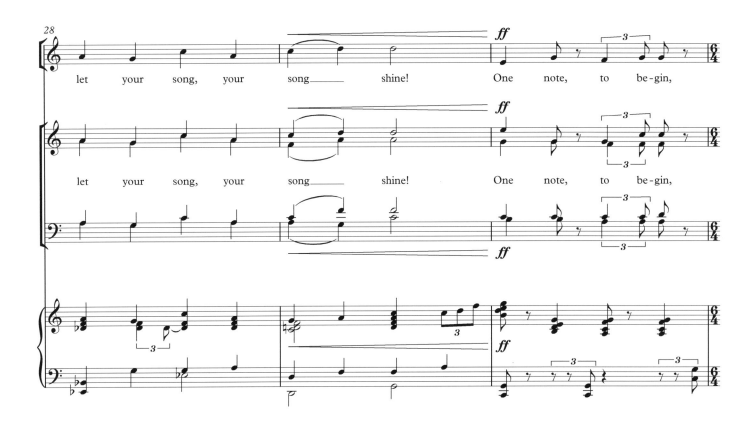

let the light in. One note, now's the time, let your song

let the light in. One note, now's the time, let your song

shine! Let your song shine, let your

shine! Let your song shine, let your

108

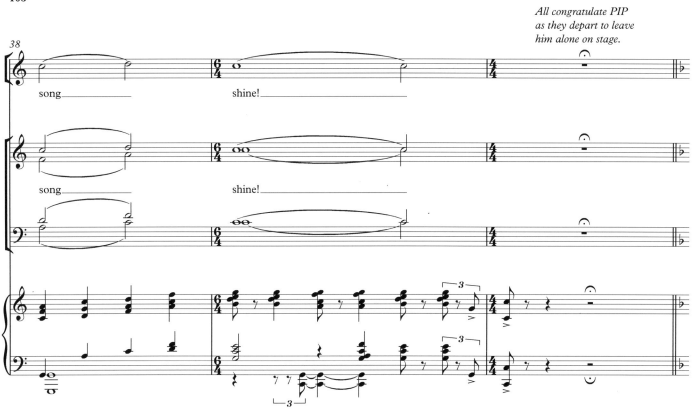

All congratulate PIP as they depart to leave him alone on stage.

17. Epilogue
(Pip)

All I real-ly came to show is how what lies be-neath can grow. And

how some-times the stran-gest mouth can let de-light-ful mu - sic out.

a little slower ♩ = 76

What-ev - er else you take a - way, re-

-mem-ber how we sang to - day. And in the si-lence of your heart,

rit.

"Start."

let the heal - ing mu - sic

(*p*)